TIME INTERLOPER

Also by Trevor Heim-Prechter

poetry

NINE DAYS AGO

Time Interloper

Trevor Heim-Prechter

Heim-Prechter Publishing
2018

First Printing: 2018

ISBN: 978-0-692-16150-0

To Grant Morrison

For showing me inclusion.

Contents

Prose

Staggering, I breathe the fading autumn air.
A month, I have stood here, passing by the
Peoples' beings. I know them to be the backdrop.

The newly developed supports in my piece
Are humans for which have a background
Of their own. I detail them with each chapter.

Is this the sequel to my original? Or perhaps,
The novel has only begun: waltzing in on a fresh
Beginning sentence. I hope it to be best-selling.

November 7, 2017

Soul and the Orchestra

For Audrey Nowak

I

Expression—
Captured in a few short
Minutes.

The grand woman
Bounces like a top,
Her wings spreading out,

The heat of the air
Touching all those
Around her.

I am a mere
Observer,
Taking in memories

I can't remember.
The faces
Of a thousand instruments

Bleed
Indistinguishable moments.
I know they have more to come.

Memories
Are a language
Which can never be translated.

I,
From the seats away,
Cannot bellow the notes

I have played.
They are communicating
In their singular space,

And I am witnessing
Their feelings being
Danced to, without a trace.

II

Weeks ago,
I visited a song
That was rests to me previously.

She, though,
Was a cello,
And I, the stand.

III

Still,
I am fascinated by
A position for which

I stood,
My back arched,
And the audience

On the other side
Of my one-way
Voice.

He,
The boy to match
My rhythm,

Sat with me
Through those moments
Of gesture.

We pawned
A chessboard
To people who knew

Not English.
I was content
With logic's sound.

5

IV

The largest tiny
Piece I ever
Tasted

Was on a trip
To fool's land.
It was a lollipop,

And it had the flavor
Of discontent and
Grass.

Though,
Another gave me
Assortments of candy,

Things that
Stripped away
The dry texture.

My epiphany:
He was a store owner,
Making sure his customer

Was not upset,
So he would
Never be sued.

6

The sweets
Were awe,
However.

V

Before all,
Chicago blazed
With my laughter.

Before that,
I was an individual,
Standing among an orchestra,

Attempting to sing.
I was off,
Little can I say.

And way back,
I met a bass clef.
She . . . he . . . we . . .

Died with tones
Together.
Music, as they say.

All of these miniature
Lines, born from
A moment

Where I saw a person
I deemed "fame"
And I wanted to mimic.

VI

Communication
Will never show simple sound
To the youth masses.

June 20, 2018

Denial

My dog knows not the elementary build
I routinely walk. He sits, bored, in the
Shade of a tree. I, too, sit bored in shade.

He was found on streets, streets I assume I
Will never be familiar with. What
Does he long for? (And what do you often

Write for?) I search, I say. (What for, *person*?)
To dwell and capture pictures, other forms
Of art could not. (Stupid, wasteful use of

Time.) No, I must live out my head, it says
To do so. Those cards that I feel need be
Played, to be gambled on. To speak the truth.

(I only wish to be entertained, please.)
I understand, I am here (in your head.)
Yes, but here in physical form as well.

(To play? To play?) For minutes, I suppose.
(No.) I must commit to my passion, though.
(Me first, yourself second, my dear *person*.)

May 16, 2018

Memory Lane

A road departed from the one
We were driving on. You laughed, wheeling
Us back in the direction of that ironically

Named place. To our disappointment, it was
A short-lived experience, ending in a cul-de-sac
A few feet after the very sign of "Memory Ln."

So, you whirled us in a circle, a slow doughnut,
And we giggled about the years that had come
Prior. They were sugar veins leading up to a bond,

A bond for which the both of us could laugh
About—spinning around in the center of cute
Houses. Let all of our common background

Come floating in the center of a dead end
Street. Let them birth there and grow, until
We become so sick with longing that we drown

In all the happy times.

May 17, 2018

A Moment I Wanted to Capture in Words

White encrusted raindrops fall
Aimlessly in the morning night.
The pavement deepens in its corners
Where waters reign. Undisturbed,

The lamplights talk across the touched
Landscape. No amount of life or words
Could ever encapsulate the crisp, cold
Grip the air has on my neck. And I know

As the winter fades—heavy into liquid—
It will be forgotten on my sleep. So,
I take in his filthy churning breath, and
Watch as the scenery sits in pictures.

March 30, 2018

Summer, Ten Years Ago

The porch is salty hot,
And when I reach inside—
That glass door opening so thin—
I find myself fancied by a white, spinning
Fan: it's air rushing, seizing

A current in my house,
Up, and through the stairwell
That leads to my bedroom.

A baby blue wall,
Stained with areas
Of child's print. My brother
Broke my bed while
Jumping, and I never
Forgave him.

This house,
With its chill and
Its exterior heat,
I ache to open
That door once more,
To know how the new

Residents have
Decorated it now,
To guide the air through
Their own lives, and feel
As my olden summer gives
Them goosebumps and a frigid
Sight of two

Boys hopping across
A mattress,
A mattress with blue
Covers and a blue
Happiness that

Faded with the Julys
Since.

May 29, 2018

Set-Up

She, her dark locks fitted
Tight with a color hat,
Passed my horizon, too.

What un-wrote music came
To this land to dance through
Our unmet selves and guide

Us to meet, ever so
Briefly? She went on to
The sun, disappearing.

March 7, 2018

Lunch After Class

What moments are so
Poignant that they bulge
In the fabric of my past?

Why is it that this table, with
Its mundane existence,
Will never pick up speed

From years tomorrow?
Their voices are soaked
In fruit. Let me hear them forever.

March 27, 2018

Ice Walking

There's a streak,
Separating the right side
Of the snow and the left.
People walk the middle—

Their feet grazing the frozen
Material in the side banks.
The safe road: a pathway for
Which no one can flirt with.

I tremble, dancing my toes
Across the rigid aisle. It smells
Of daring adventures, grim promises.
To the right, I keep my body, swaying,

Watching the others stare onward
To their next feat. But it is me who
crunches down on the temporary land.
It exhausts on my weight—screaming.

January 26, 2018

Time Interloper

I

The ticking that runs through situations
Had quite a purple stomach ache one fine
Century ago. *It* was a scared boy,

Who ran through the dry chips of a playground
Away from these god-awful children, their
Dripping, dribbling bodies smelling of piss.

Time could not handle the scent of these two:
The bodily and the coward. So, *She*
Sank them to a place they could not annoy:

The *Outreaches of Space*, o, a place where
They would fade to nothing. However, the
Small, scared boy fell further in the abyss.

He woke to an older sun, his face numb.
This was escape: to wake in other times,
A chase endured for centuries to come.

January 11, 2018

Lives

If there are such things as past lives,
Then I must have been
Happy in my prior.

I can feel it in the way
I dawn on its
Nostalgia.

I miss it so.

October 14, 2017

Staring Back

For Elizabeth Walder

New Days eat things
That don't exist. I met
A Thursday once and
He was addicted to scents
Of childhood:

His favorite being the holidays.
With them, the Thursday
Defecated beautiful, morose
Memories and fed them,
Forcefully, to all those

Nearby. They gagged on
What once was. He is
Nothing compared to
Saturdays, however,
Those beasts yearn for

The taste of loneliness,
And devour all persons
Who munch on old photographs
Of happiness and ignited
Parties. It is Days

Like these that are most
Vicious. They take the
Newest of sights and mend
Them to blinding past moments,
Even ones without a friend.

December 30, 2017

Nostalgia

I want the forced warmth
Of winter, again. Gimme
The late-night times with
Friends as we order pizza

Next to a feigned red tree.
I want the feeling of winter
Mornings when the storm
Hits unexpectedly.

I want to wander in the
Glittering masterpiece
Of the cloaked, sprinkling
Lawns of snowy *nuit.*

July 14, 2017

Tea

For Linda Prechter

Genuine moments taste shortly
Of leaves. Liquids that are
So clear in my throat give the
Late night a definition. I smile

During the boredom of a
Wednesday. Today is a day
forgotten, but it is a day
I experience for quite a while.

January 3, 2018

Lovely Sentences

She wrote in lovely sentences, that girl.
She said that her words were not poetry.

I told her, "nay, your depth is more than that.
You speak voice as if you were the wind's whirl.

English never needed to make some sense.
It is merely the definitions' carol.

The choir will wait 'til the notes are fresh.
Then, comes the allure: their sweet harmony."

The way she would doubt, it beat me quite blue.
"Trust your one mind, it has stories to tell."

You can create narratives of pastel.

May 24, 2018

Sights in English

Parting down the left,
Its face twitches with
Smooth snow. It dances
With the tuff atop (left).

A structure, holding itself,
Clothed with
Storms—all that enchant
A widening, plump smile.

Its lips balance—as if
They were weighted down
By the two large bulbs
For which its entrance

Shines. How evil the above
Must be to give such
Beauty an imperfect way
To see the light.

November 30, 2017

Potted

For once, I came across
A painted vase—all
Filled with flowers.
(Roses and all other beautiful plants)

It faded—quick—into the
Transparent night. Liquor
Liquid snuffed out.
(Leaves and all)

I tasted the dotted
Paint as I tongued
The air.
(It was silver with violet)

Phlegm, in the dark,
I witnessed a
Warped vase.
(The same, but different)

I was not a spectator
Of its contents, rather
The flavored art.
(I wish to plant)

September 14, 2017

I Am My Cat

She must think the same as I,
With her feline-self striding.

I know. My elaborate self has
Read great works, experienced

Other minds. What is a cat brain
Compared to the best writers

Of humankind? Surely, with
Stretches and many flexes of

Literature I will be able to flow
Into the many minds I have

Never been. Who have
I been other than I? A casing

Trapped within the barriers
Of myself, and soon her.

May 2, 2018

Dreams of Something Else

April's crisp desire for
Winter (she adores her so),
Gave way this year,

I saw it plain: the month had
Descending abiotic
Sheep covering

The ground. And there, in the field,
There was a counting, counting for
The days to come.

(They did.) Like whispering, I
was reminded of nights in
Tennessee—where

May was so vain, so brutal
With delicious lips. Thoughts
Of December

Were forgot. When two seasons
Touch so abrupt, the sinking
Thoughts do surface.

April 23, 2018

Fantasy

Your elastic nature bewitches the fairies,
They gape at your kingdom—its fantastic scopes,
Spreading to distances beyond imagination.

Those tiny humanoids dance on the extended
Royalty, their chests thriving on juicy berries,
Enchanted kindness. And they are blessed

With jewelry, with addictive saliva. (*Your lips
Are bonsai trees*, the fairies giggled.) Flowers,
Weeds, and scuttling creatures all feverishly

Live inside you. They all prance as they do
In tales only found in forgotten novels,
Where their people blessed the very leaves

That make your nose, your dewdrop hair.
Internally, your labyrinth is made of spirited
Winds, they speak of that central river—

She must be so pretty, the fairies wonder
Where on your maps does she lie. Legend
Tells of her snaking down through the south.

Her water lives in your branches, feeding all
Those who gaze your fields up and down,
Never to wonder where their town once was.

May 1, 2018

Island

From the palms of the palms,
And the sand in the sand,
And the waves atop the waves,

I am stowed away on your island,
And your island has stowed away me.

The cosmos all know
That the heat's persistence
And the cold's tranquility
And the eye's deception
And the nose's obsession,

All brought me here
On the water's shore,
And that the water's shore
Brought me here as well.

For, I have discovered your island,
And your island has taken me captive.

May 25, 2018

Children's Story

Do you speak of me
To your friends? I reference
You as though you were

A book I read in my
Childhood. I speak
Of the wonder you

Gave and still
Continue to give.
Do you do the same?

July 12, 2017

My Foot

Those legs below my torso
Were buried in my stare. I
Kept it there for safekeeping.

My ankles were chained tight
To my lucid tongue. Yet, I hoped
The words would escape my weeping.

They unfolded quick into air,
And you left me with silence,
For which will haunt my sleeping.

November 26, 2017

Those Pauses

There was this
Undeniable silence
As I sung my
Vaporous being
Away.

You knew
No words
To which to
Respond,

And I wept
For you to
Capture my pleas:

They leapt through
The valleys my fingertips
Couldn't reach.

Simply,
You wouldn't,

And in that
I knew.

September 21, 2017

Idolization

"Your brass base
Ate my inner iris
The day our distance
Shattered.

The city you danced in,
It roared with sky-touching
Equals. I watched them
From the horizon.

I stood, gazing.
Rainstorms broke
The banks around
Your star-dazzling

Home," (Why did I think
You'd choose me over
The buildings?)
I wept aloud.

October 4, 2017

Your Partner

A whisper in the masses:
"Someone new, someone new."
I feel my pupils focus, and then
They blink—

My staring is but an unending
Conversation, for which you
Don't partake.

I know you'll be back—
My personal landscape
Is absent and grey.

You'll have to turn away,
I know, I know,
You'll see my face—

It must be so swollen,
The way I don't let out breath.
My rhythm has no pace.

November 13, 2017

Muse

Museums were set ablaze—
Their foundations crumbled and
My being watched as they streaked
Against the night sky.

The sweet crinkle of painted
Canvas illuminated my joy.
The dozens around watched
And fainted—their history lost to smoke.

My being could see her kisses
And you on the museum's steps—
Frozen like a photograph.
And here—on that night—the

Kisses burnt to ruins. Laughter.
Laughter. There was glee, o,
Yes, all viewers only saw the yellow
And orange, but it was my being

That danced on the embers
Of your memory. Each ash
Tasted like your insides—
What a beautiful art piece

My being has created. It
Boils emotion far and wide—
This model of pure inspiration.
Give me more, give me more.

November 12, 2017

Moments I Wanted to Share

The lights around you flicker,
That's the way I picture it,
Your thin lips pucker, thicker,

Meet with a pretty other:
A moment I can't be there,
A moment that does smother.

Your confidence and hips sway,
Your character grows to lengths.
I'm absent from you today.

Bitter, stubborn, I'm beaten.
I can't witness those pieces,
Those junctures have me eaten.

Hung up. Why is it unfair?
Can't be here. I want nothing
More than for you to share.

June 15, 2018

Jealousy

(Tethered)
The elephant's ivory tusks
Wail among the pouring
Humans, all screaming—

(Touched)
The creature can see,
Past the little tips of hands,
A safari—fruiting with must.

(Transparency)
Centering the frame,
A vision is so blurred,
The elephant's trunk reaches—

(Thirst)
A flowing, drowning
Tower raining down on the non-
Human crowds—in the distance.

(Taunted)
The beast had traveled east
To live a dream of circuses,
But his home has found other.

(Trauma)
The rope tangles 'round the pole,
Humans cheer to the entertainment
Of a giant heat—without home's role.

(Tired)
The elephant supposes home
Must have a
Circus of their own.

November 15, 2017

Time Interloper

II

His voice was at that awkward middle part,
Where he could not quite finish a sentence,
When he stumbled upon that stupid school.

Time walked *Her* fingertips through cabinets.
Somewhere within *Her* files, *She* knew *She*
Would find that wretched ache, whenever be.

Though, he was hidden in the ugliest
Of places, where masculine beasts fed on
Humiliation, and only did rule.

Two-thousand one, the small, scared boy drifted
From voice to voice, hiding from the male beasts.
Difficulty, he avoided the fee

Of being not from there, not from when. *Time,*
Though, snatched him quick when he was not looking.
And thus, he faltered in his *ever* climb.

February 27, 2018

Advertisement

In conversation, your epitome is so simple,
You must stink of a strawberry flavor,

Songs must follow your trail, your feet,
Your prints. Promotion must be written in

Watermelon text, the font reaching
All who desire a simple, kind

Product, sale.

May 14, 2018

They Asked Me to Dance with Their Partner

Friend,
Can you imagine the soft coal
In the air?

Here,
They say it roars, with flappers and all,
Their souls bare.

I wish
To tumble across these whispered parties,
My complex attire whirling.

Yet,
The coal still burns, I see it screech!
O, my lucid eyes burn.

They say
To distract myself with the songs;
How can many be so stubborn?

Whenever
My vehicle comes close to those
Mountains,

My tipsy stomach
Bleeds filtered bile.
I sick out my window.

No matter the amount of
Beauty, I can never not see the
Smoke in the distance.

July 11, 2018

Horror, Your Horror

Compel me to not lurk underneath your bed.
O, my scales scathe the wooden boards holding
Your mattress up, holding it away from

My teeth: the way saliva creates webs between
Each knife molar; they have taste buds of their own.
And I desire the compulsive poison they call your flesh.

The closet: I do not stand there, but even there, it be.
It has no teeth, yet you cower, blanket and all,
Staring at that thing that isn't me.

If I am a werewolf, you are my moon.
In this form, I wish to snuff the night sky.
But during the time of sol, I am a bear atop

Your sleep. Why do you fear me? Why
Must you knock me to the floor,
Where I rot to my mummified being?

There, you twirl to the light's cover:
It takes away that door in the corner,
And I am merely a teddy hidden underneath.

June 19, 2018

The Grave Woke Weeks Ago

Birthed: it came out like a rotting corpse.
Stringing bits of drool broke from
Its jaw, gnawing, gnawing, cobweb
Eyes straining for a blood-pumping
Feeling. Saw a copper plaque:

A name written for which the
Body knew only awe. Nimble
Bones ached to the
Promise—that of
A human's warm touch, and

Its shivering soul streamed
Once more. Smoldering. The
Dead longs. Surely, with its
Rot, the creature did
Stir, beckoning toward the

Idea. Open, close, its grip faltered,
Falters still. Draining, the fleshless
Figure shifted not, a repetitious snap
Of dried, dried lips did tongue the surface
Often. Died: never still.

April 18, 2018

Obsession

Cure this involuntary pulse,
I am so quick to imagine a
Scenario I wish not to see.

Correct my inner reality,
Tell me it is wrong, tell me it is
Wrong. The possibility

Of the sun-kissed sky
Swallowing ornate planets
Is surely close to none,

Remind me that my
Mind is sick with a yellow
Toad, and that you would

Never flash written word
To the speckled valley
Ceiling. Please, tell me,

My dear, that I am walling
Myself in an asylum of untrue
Situations, and that you would

Never trace your pace over
The roots of a wicked, wicked
Position. Heal me, free me.

May 18, 2018

Anger

Creation of a new form of art:
One for which I cannot even
Begin to describe in English words.

And in this art, I, *per se*, paint myself
To be standing in a circular group
Of humans, all chanting my name.

(Now, this vision can be seen with song,
And heard with chalk scribbles on a teacher's
Board. Art is so flexible.)

In this crowd, I wander forward, and—
What's this?
The piece, the project, the colors,

The structure, the feel, the texture,
The stains, the setting, the smell . . .
It has gone beyond what I have imagined

It to be. My fingers, my mind, my
Mouth cannot completely comprehend
How this work of creativity is made

Or started. It just is. And now, it bends
On its own. It is more than just an image or
A scene. It is depth. It is both the day

I drove home, letting out all of the sounds
That my lungs could possibly conceive,
And the evening I melted into

My dorm bed, raining out pigments
And pigments of all the broken
Lightbulbs that lived inside me.

The canvas became a dot of singularity,
That held me so tight. And I was (so, so)
Scared of losing it. Of losing that moment,

That strange, awkward afternoon I said
Goodbye to it, the artwork I dreamed of.
I stabbed a paper, knowing that

The reds and the purples and the blues
That came with it, my craft, my design,
Would never be able to be replicated.

It was breathing with the mountains,
Transforming with the birth of children,
And leaving my out-lashing animation.

(From it, as all art does, came inspiration.)
Creators mixed the splattered adjectives,
And my novel, my film became an idea

I never had. (It blended with other parts
Of a spectrum.) And I find myself desiring
Back the pastels and the lights.

I have promoted myself to the all-knowing
Form of sight. Here, despite having all,
I wish to have the simple work of

Living: to conga with a photograph again,
To act with clay, and to sing with sculptures
Of peoples before.

Stop. Stop. I must know why I crave such
Cracked cuisines. There is no need to
Dive into such expressions any further.

I wish I could rid myself of these details.
I am so tired of aching. (This congregation,
It ties together so well, with two individuals

Standing at my feet. Their scent:) A feel-good
Fire of alteration. I know not the tonality, nor will I
name this nasty and narcotic, never-noble print of

Excrement. This now-sentient art has risen far
Above its artist. It was never the intention to
Include such a mind in the turning legacy.

May 23, 2018

Withdrawals and Other Pains

Replicate, dearest,
Replicate those rhymes
I have sketched
Out for you. Please,
Forgive all that I have

Pronounced to you. Just
Replicate them well, and
Never glance back. I am
Smoking
Depths I have gifted you.

Whether through my
Nostrils, mouth, veins,
Or whatever else, I have
Yet to find that replication,
To find a way out.

June 9, 2018

Two AM

A voice kept me up
Last night. And I supposed
That—just for one night—
I could be the princess.

The ballroom's ring had
Sung evenings and evenings
Prior. (I don't suppose it ever
Stopped. How do you make it

Stop?) I grow ever so tired,
Falling to sleep's trance much
After intended. The prince
Keeps me dancing so.

March 18, 2018

Self

Pleading. This same season has gone on long.
It's not quite snowing, it's not quite falling,
No, it's not even sunny or rainy.

There are caving-in mounds around myself;
They have a pull, a yank to which I saw.
There goes Kansas, right down the bottomless.

Vomit. That thing, that stab wound in my mouth.
Up comes trees, houses, and a herd or two.
Beaming, they rattle off one another.

I, as well, do travel down this damn loop,
Seeing more rocks and craters the whole way,
Not once meeting the end, the closing point,

It's a circular slide for gobbled shit,
Washing my bare stomach, my bulbous head.
"Feed the monster," I dare those who enter.

May 15, 2018

Thinking Again

Coo, my basement bed stutters,
Attempting a solution.
It summons willows, quite green.
They are acquainted with song,
Telling me: cease your shudders.

Is this the foreseen red spring?
How has the foreign salt rains
Cured my trembles, fixed my flesh?
They can't. My blankets are locked,
Chained to my repeat quiver.

Flight, the mattress takes shivers,
Illusionary, raw leaves,
These things take me to battle,
To damp dungeons where I shake.
Cursed be of my constant wake.

June 4, 2018

Napalm

Echo: the lobe bleeds out
Over my face. It reeks of the
Days and nights prior.

Echo, again: I race through
The woods, my howls bluntly
Shaking my skull.

Echo, once more: no matter
How hard I scrub, it won't remove.
And my body seems to produce more.

December 7, 2017

Stubborn

We must be willing to work
Through tough dynamics
To make things work.

Families eat atop this picnic table—
What fertilizer grew them to be so . . .?

O, I haven't a word that could begin to dissect,
To showcase the way they started in the womb,
And met along the intersections.

My own moon cannot part from this gravity.
It craves simple sandwiches and chips,
The things picket-fenced families eat.
How simple, how by-the-book.

We are wandering in a galaxy I wish not to be.

My crater-nails are sinking into this separation,
Desiring to take down the barricade of wood.

Free me, please, take this glowing body
Out from my rogue sphere. I will never cease
Until my picnic-destroying hands are cut clean.

July 19, 2018

Decision, Delusion

Five feet away from my person,
There lies a motionless baby bird,
Shaded by a tree, a tree without choice.

Five feet from its trunk,
I am fed yellow from the
Transparent above.

The stalk in the distance
Creeps, unknowing its inability
To deter from simple destiny.

I am unscathed by the wind,
The forward way nature develops,
I struggle with the frothy insides,

How my engine marries complexities.
O, I wish to be taken by the invisible
Dancer that is the matter around me.

How simple it is to stretch my arms
And be clasped by the fury of skies
And cut short by the ground below!

Why must I be cursed with mind?
To know how other natural developments
Are affected by my choice—my evil right.

We are gods next to the coward,
Straightforward way of living.
My thoughts are sour with fright.

July 8, 2018

The Color Yellow

Lemon.
The fleshy
Taste dips my tongue.

Two of them.
I feel quite
Sick, my eyes run.

Gold.
The thing that
Comforts me after.

I say,
No more, I can't,
And bees prickle

My external
With warmth, a fire
That is like the star

In the east, and then
The west. Sol, they
Say, but I say it

Burns flesh.
I have desired
Yellow since I first

Can remember,
And now I think
Of how crunchy

That amber is.
It isn't butter or
Cheese, it is

A pain
That is as good as
Lemon.

May 28, 2018

Dull Fruit

Peel it, and trace its
Simple veins with the
Tip of your blade. Tell
Me over how important
This product must be.

By the first week, I
Grasp it. I do. By
The fifteenth, I'm
Bored of the seeds,
Of the outer skin,

Of the way it grows.
Yes, nature's abundance
Has plentiful beauty,
But what does my
Expanding knowledge

Gain? It's vermillion, yes,
It's fed the thirst of
Millions, yes, but I
Desire the related
Meals, the mouth-staining

Sides. This wet sphere is
A basis, a foundation of
The bountiful feast,
The tasteful hunt,
My true desire.

April 25, 2018

Big

The columns of darkness are streaking
With weaving plants, their bodies streaming
Like horizontal rain. I lurk between the poles,
Scratching my fingertips against their base.
He's here, in the terrain of a million whispers.

The feline nearby dips her paw into the below,
And is whisked away by shadows. I trail her tail,
Best as I can, but only find myself churning the
Same path as before. The thick's many spines
Catch the corner of my eye . . . *he's here* . . .

Among the many bony features, between the ribs,
And the digested fur, his scent lingers. He drifts
From the wolves (how they must do the same).
The Skeletal, The Skeletal, the way he knows
The innards of the bodies. His pillar fingers

Root themselves, carving my own back with
Dreaded chills. I open, cracking as if a cocoon,
Releasing his fluttering snack. And out I slide.
He takes me well, murmuring the rigid secrets,
And I collapse into his fleshy cavity.

February 15, 2018

A River Asks for Advice

The essence told the river to spit back.
When time arrived, the waters would be one.
Then, the offer came much like an attack.
Temptation flooded; its banks overrun.

July 10, 2018

Bad Hair

A tight hat encapsulates
The top of my skull,

(The wet of my
Locks are wilting
In the bore of class.)

And once I remove it,
my petals unravel.

December 5, 2017

Letters to Flight

I

Dear Flight,

Cacophonous wonders are bleeding out
From that slit in my side temple you sliced.
I've lost feeling in my fingers and doubt.

Sincerely,

A Concussing Individual

II

Dear Flight,

When will you bring that bandage you promised?
I don't know how long I can last without.
O, it hurts, I thought you were one to trust.

Sincerely,

A Concussing Individual

III

Dear Flight,

I hear—through whispers—you're a doctor now.
You fix all those women and men quite well.
I guess I healed over time, anyhow.

Sincerely,

A Concussing Individual

IV

Dear Flight,

You should see the scar on my bulbous face.
I did as they told, and placed ointments there,
Soon, the mark will be gone without a trace.

Sincerely,

A Concussing Individual

V

Dear Flight,

I hope your wings have flown far and quite well.
Waiting for you is the game I play now:
A response, I hope; only time will tell.

Sincerely,

A Concussing Individual

VI

Dear Flight,

Where your talons have touched, the scar remains.
I long for your letters, your touch, your grace.
Honest, as years go by, everything pains.

Sincerely,

A Concussing Individual

VII

Dear Flight,

They, the people around town, call me freak.
Knowing of my longing for your feathers,
They have tarred me and gifted me a beak.

Sincerely,

Freak (A Concussing Individual)

VIII

Dear Flight,

Even I doubt you were reality.
I thought you'd migrate back to my hometown,
But now even that small thought is set free.

Sincerely,

Freak

IX

Dear Flight,

Please return as you said you one day would.
The townsfolk don't even glance me an eye.
Thought you said you were only ever good.

Sincerely,

Freak

X

Dear Flight,

The tar—eight months now—has been in my eye.
Perhaps, if I take the wind, I'll find you.
For now, I glide through blue. This is goodbye.

Sincerely,

Freak

June 18, 2018

Time Interloper

III

She set his feet where the music mingled
Between the seconds. There were smiles here.
They invited and dismissed as they pleased.

The sun broke between its winds. *She* knew he
Would be devoured by its static teeth,
Tearing his flesh and bone into stringed meat.

A constellation took the man's hand well,
And, together, they square stepped through molars.
Like floss within scattered lights, the two eased

An escape from the damaged, reflective
Mouths edged in the *Outreaches of Space.* See,
The Greatest Star of them all broke its feet;

It toppled down, roaring like a rogue spell:
The Earth did end. The man's lips eaten by
The other smiles and he sent to hell.

March 29, 2018

Auto-cannibalism

Damn me. Take my acid
Mind and dine with
The previous impulses
I've etched into

The un-soft earth. Damn me,
I say, damn me.
Unimaginable gore
Must await all,

Descriptions with horrid,
Horrid lore. I
Will be there for centuries
More, bodily

Insides finger-painted
On my forehead,
Drills bellowing, my frontal
Lobe saying "damn

"Me." Damn me. Damn me. Damn
Me. Damn me. Damn
Me. Damn me. Damn me. Damn me.
Damn me. Damn me.

April 6, 2018

Chest

Hamlet knows my bare composition.
His attraction for me
Is felt in his royal fingers,

Scribing soliloquies—sweet stabs
Into the field around my dairy.
O, his arms stirred sea pirates

To noble castle walls,
Where I stiffened, feeling the rub
Of his stoic king.

Be as it be,
I bathe where she fell,
And though the prince knew,

He lets me wander her grounds,
Singing the songs she plucked there.
Why must I turn mad at her grave?

With his broken crown, he waits atop,
Knowing I sink myself in her soil.
I whisper for her to speak in spirits,

But she does not.
Her skull gives no response,
And yet I voice her so.

I don't speak death fluently;
I can't translate all her thoughts.
All I know is she silent to my woe.

Yet, again, his pulsing touch
Reminds me of her memory.
I shout this at the headstone.

To be hung by the dead
Or to trace Hamlet's final act,
I question, I question.

July 15, 2018

Death in the Family

An inner lining bit of flesh
Hardens when it reaches
My left chest. I clench my

Jaw. Hereditary traits are
But every human's Achilles
Heel. And here I sit, too

Overworked by the meaning
Behind these bodily workings
To see the pain it has caused

Others. Cyclical, perhaps,
Selfish tendencies will pass
On as well, and my suffering

Will be a mere footnote
In my descendants' woeful
pleas to their genes.

January 2, 2018

Nerve Pains

—a gorge through my palm,
naked.

Everywhere I walk
New cavities form
To the beat of my toes
Against the glass shards.

May 25, 2017

In the Morning

Feverishly, my gust surfaces
To my loft, it develops
And grows. With elegance,
It glides and adds matter

To its body. There is a
Wonder to the way it
Limps—tired—unable
To reach for the door—

The gust, guided by the
Winds, seizes the knob,
And continues as always:
Drifting about the day.

February 5, 2018

Bargaining

Please,
I'll do anything,
Fix my portrait, my smile.
It seems so crooked
In the fluorescent light.
How are admirers supposed
To admire with such an ugly sight?

June 13, 2018

Two Nights

Secrets: a delicious recipe
That spoke of a thief's plan.
Only her partners knew the
Way she entered.

As they recounted later,
It was with great care
And much hush. No one knew
That impossible place like her.

Her husband lacked knowledge
Of the fresh shift in life;
Only that one night his wife
Was somber, and the next—and many

After—she was ecstatic. She
Offed her partners
Well. Their silences—
She finished her dream.

Her husband; a call.
Ariiing, Ariiing: A petty crime
Transformed into murders.
Victims after victim, came his sister

And many others. The town swept by
Voice; No one noticed a
Robbery blanketed in silence.
The husband, with all of his riches and wife,

Grew to find that his nights
Were filled with confusion and doubt,
As many of the townsfolk knew
All too well.

May 27, 2018

Stolen

An artist translates her whim
To the paper—it's glorious!
It's misunderstood! How it
Does stain the eyes with color.

Thieves! Their rat-like faces scoop
Up her ideas without a
Blink. "Artists" shed their skin to
Become anew, rat skin on

The floor. Her brethren are
Rodents like her. Disgust, dirt,
And creativity. Her
Whim is translated to all.

February 6, 2018

Short Lived

Entranced, my inner-city teases
My perspective. I am but
Cognitive streets unable to
Truly touch the universe and
Its substance. And there,

On those roads, I often
Listen to tastes made up
Of unnamed chemicals. A city
Made from senses the
Human body can't feel.

So, when the outer spaces
Chose to destroy me, my
Citizens will be encapsulated in dark:
A static, unknowing black,
One for which shall never remember itself.

April 27, 2018

Figment

Quaking, the landscape is unbearably dry.
And to my disappointment, no matter how much
I shout my fucking voice out to the horizon,
The grass won't grow back. My chucks

Pick up the dirt and the dust and the sand
All too often, and I know, I just know, that
The foliage I love doesn't have a heart or
Mind that can be compared to my own.

I can only begin to have a basic understanding
Of how a deity could write a story so small
And meaningless. All the great authors write
Of words that segment my brain into two.

But this figment, that transcends all of time,
Could never grow the world the way
I wish it to be. And I want it so bad. To crack
The waves and to shatter air. I want all

Inhuman things. To magnetize the rubble,
And strangle away all opposing obstacles.
Change, damnit, change. The trees are
All dying, and I can do nothing but watch.

February 13, 2018

Sleuths Searching

Much like an eternal star,
There is a house that burns
Without a single falter,
And it is said that those who
Mingle with mystery are found
On its grounds, searching.

Damn be them for trying.
Damn be them for wanting,
For searching for that ultimate
Prize. If one finds the answer,
The answer to why that house
Started to burn, burn eternally,

I will be relieved, satisfied.
However, to their unknowing
Knowledge, I am the clue for
Which they have dedicated
Themselves to. I sit, calm,
On the pavement, next to the lot.

Weeks pass, where I gleam
In the twinkle of the fire,
And a man comes casting by,
He discovers my hints—my evidence.
His notice, his analysis,
They are but the dose of curiosity

For which I long.
He stashes me away in his pocket,
And I am a trinket for him to think over,
To dissect. Yet, to my dismay,
He never stops pacing that lot,
For which that fire burns.

I hear him mutter,
Often with much confusion,
Ignoring how I am the last piece
To reveal the cause of that smoldering
Ash. The man keeps washing over
That same junk, those same lost clues.

July 3, 2018

Depression

She told me to write how I feel.

I am atop a mountain, where I see all clear,
And all smudged. The celestial beings that swayed
To my flesh's tune are all selfish in the clouds below me.

Those fragments only see my acne. The way they converse,
One might think the bumps across my skin are war,
What sort of murder has my beauty committed?

O, I attempt to build snow castles to complement
Their heavenly statue. One should see the shimmer of
White, the iridescent sight!

Yet, they call out to the wind, to their city,
That I am a scrawny form, not that of a perfect build.
"I . . . thought I was one of you."

It seems as though the mist within the mountainous skyline
Is merely just laughter, laughter directed at my attempts
To be with them.

I am mortal, and I choke on this oxygen up here.
I can't tell, but I imagine they do not glance as I roll
Down the slope aside them. My carcass,

With its stretches and its stunted view,
Joins those who decayed at the thought of
Being with the falsified gods.

June 16, 2018

Sir Oddity

I am quite used to it,
Those questions that emit.
I deal with them—

They are shaped like dissection tools, their hands
Probing my unease stance,
My fever brain.

Today, the shower
Cleansed my rashes
Gone,

But once I exited,
My cousin,
His eyes on my flu,

Asked me again,
Those questions
I often knew.

His grin was edged
With giggles, entertaining
My cough and my phlegm.

I suppose, with the amount I get,
I should set a charge
To question, to prod, to view.

To answer them all:
Yes, this is my disease,
I was born with it well.

One day my passion
Will stop, and I will
Lie frozen with it in my chest.

Laughter
is in voice; I hear it in silence.
You cannot hide it in your questions.

You cannot hide in compliments.
You cannot hide it at all.
You think me not normal,

And that's all I will ever know.
Even in my family,
I am an oddity to show.

July 10, 2018

Small

What rigid breath is sewn into my skin?
I sit. Alone. My room is a falter
Within the whole scheme of the solar rings.

I live in the casing of my bare flesh,
Cursed to endure the kindness that flares
Among others, the kindling eating

My awe. It is in these moments that I
Sink down low onto my floor, feeling the
Carpet's muscle. And beyond that, I fall.

Underneath the flooring of myself is
Where I float, legs curled to my chest, and my
Head bowed, drowning in their full tenderness.

March 1, 2018

Common Conversations

"O, I do so adore your ugly face.
It glints unique, disfigured with beauty.
If I were you, I'd snatch your visage so.
It would be like a red living painting,
I could walk as a museum, with art curves."

Take it. Round your paintbrushes on my edge.
Watch as my chin curls like paper, rippled.
I'm sure in this given moment you'd live,
You'd be art, truly. Without birth, it's true.
It's unique. Maybe bearable for you.

April 30, 2018

Away

My crib has many walls, I see them all.
Human One and Human Two pop in for a view,
I giggle at their mighty noses.

But fear I know, when they disappear.
O, what horror my lonely world is now
Without another to share my existence!

A-ha, though, Human Two comes back,
She gives me raw food and a new diaper, too.
I form a grin to give her thanks,

But in return she floats beyond my walls!
I dribble, I gasp, how will I ever know affection?
Please, o, please, God, form another.

And He does: Human One, who then goes.
Soon, I know that they will return.
There must be more beyond my vision.

Human One comes again, but with another:
Human Three, her face is a stutter.
Where be Two? I want her now!

O, I do learn, she comes less and less.
I bawl to one noon and the next.
One and Three come and go,

But Two I barely know.
And as the years grow, their faces
Become monsters to which I bellow.

July 11, 2018

How They Murdered Him Without Knowledge

A woman—her tongue imbued with poison.
She reached for a bat in the
Sacred temple. Its wooden features screamed
A wail—shattering the woman's control:
Taking hold, and beating the incoming
Air; to her sister's near home, she went.

Her sister—a girl bearing beauty horns.
"O, sister," the woman cried, "run to
The woods, far, for I will murder you with
This weapon." And both went. Red, white,
The sister shielded her beauty face, and
The curse struck them both.

The page—his milking ear, bleeding to, fro.
To his unfortunate end, the two girls
No longer knew (due to the curse) of their
Murderous arms, swinging with a beating
Bat. And they then thrash him bloody, *though*,
Unknowingly. Over him, they talked tea.

March 6, 2018

Swine

Betrayal. I sat in the grass open,
Staring as you and the other
Disappeared between the shaded
Trunks. My effort felt so tender there.

Gushing, what meals can I be served as?
Feed me to those who need a snack,
A passing side with scented cheese.
I am but a bit of meat,

I prepare myself for your visual please,
Waiting until the time of day is right.
Here, take your fork and knife,
Even though you prefer beef.

July 13, 2018

Venomous Clique

"Hello, Mr. Snake. Will you—
Will you share your space
With me?"

"Hello, hello, Mr. Person,
How have you been?
Welcome, welcome to
My snake pit. Say hello,
Hello to my many heads."

"Hello heads, I am simply
Searching for an area to
Be. Do you mind sharing
Your home?"

"Hello. You have been here
Before, Mr. Person."

"Yes, Mr. Snakehead, I have."

"And when, when during that
Time, that time did we tell you
To leave our pit? Oh, yes, yes,
That's right: when you were
Not a snake. You slithered like us.
You shed like us, but were you
Ever us? No. No, you were not.
You do not have our scales—"

They shout: "Our painted scales!"

"Mr. Person, sir, you did not
Have our tongues."

The heads shout: "Our sewn-in tongues!"

"But please, Mr. Person,
Come on in. This is our
Den. Isn't it nice? Look
How we mimic. Look how we
Breathe. Won't you be us? We are
Us. Are you?"

November 10, 2017

Time Interloper

IV

Ageless and winter, this place was quite faint.
Somehow, he slipped back centuries and some
To the drunken early stages of life,

Where *Time Herself* could not be. Infants ruled
Here, in this place of *was being*. And the
Small man watched as they drank themselves senseless.

"You cannot be here," they said in poor slang,
"You're naught, you're Satan." But the others did
Disagree, and within them all was strife.

One side tore at the man, and the other
Fled him to the countryside, where fire
Broke his plum body to be defenseless.

And in him he knew, beginning to end,
There was no place he belonged, for *Time* had
Mastered that well. From this, he did descend.

April 24, 2018

The Magician and His Assistant

Her trance mixed in the crowd, stale.
Sudden—the saw was lifted!
Her flavorful gasp let out.

"Show me, show me your secrets,"
She spoke, joining his one side;
A stream came to his dead drought.

Juices fed his illusions
When she watched his performance.
(Magic was real next to her.)

Though, she grew bored of the same,
Leaving the dusty old man,
His wand lifted in the blur.

Without her, the show lost taste;
The rabbit never appeared;
The lesser crowd never cheered.

July 3, 2018

Home Again

Hands trace over a photograph of myself,
They take my silhouette and detail on a new paper
To become someone else. And what was before,

Transforms into a feature someone could find in a box
Somewhere. An attic where, generations
From now, kids could stumble across

A box, where my face, with its original shades,
Could be witnessed, instead of the replacement
That has hung over the mantle for decades.

May 16, 2018

Motif

I spent all last night
Attempting to form
This poem, but no
Words seem to align
With how I felt.

Angry. Disappointed. I gave a cracked effort
Into something I cared for so dearly. The amount
Of times I rearranged that bookshelf must have
Been uncountable. At first, I did it by author's

Name, then title, then the first word in each book,
Yet nothing felt correct. No Dewey, no color, no single
Sense of organization appeased that itch, that need
For a balanced system. I guess it must have seemed

Crazy—at least to my friends—that I had expected a
Bookshelf to organize itself. Frankly, I was quite tired of
Doing all I could to upkeep it. It is not my job. I am not a
Librarian; I am a sane person, who reads. Though, as

Librarian's might think, I thought that pages could organize
Themselves. They, after all, have minds and people inside,
Why can't they do my not-job? This task, this repetitive task
Has come in and come out, day after week, and I just can't

Do it anymore. Am I insane to think such a beautiful thing
Can meet me outside of its small room? Why am I always
The one found screaming from across my house? I must
Appear so, so mad with the way I argue to that library.

I have asked it enough times to share its vocabulary,
Its literature, its wisdom. I will write pages of my own.
I don't need you. I am not a librarian, no, I am a sane
Reader, who is quite comfortable away from his shelf.

May 28, 2018

Unwanted

Riding on a constant slope toward
An audition, I devoured
Silver irises every day.

With them, my tongue bled cobble and
Stone. Stairs: they carried my soles high.
I witnessed where the horizon

Met the fleshy clouds. (They tickled.)
And through the chill I ran (and stopped,)
Disappointment, the stairs crumbled.

My building mouth falsified a
Grinning wall. He spoke (with great grit),
"Wonderful, o sky, I do adore

"The way you bright every valley."
He did slither the truth greatly,
And she knew it true. (But I was

To be the bulging atmosphere,
Not she.) O, though, she did do
Well, so stunningly tasteful. I

Had no right to want, to want, to
want the role of oxygen. (The
Sky is not mine, it is hers.)

April 17, 2018

Tarfooted Devil

She, her breasts the color of sour coins,
Dove into a lagoon of her own making.
It reeked of quiet stones and torture.

With her chiseled fingertips, she shaped
My body to her image, carving highlights
For which glare in her fractured moonlight.

You, the person who I sung novels to,
Gave her religion, a crowd to worship her.
And in a night for which I couldn't sleep,

I heard you chanting hymns with her name
Imprinted on your tar words. You walked with
Her into smoke rituals, and left me seeping.

June 14, 2018

Morning Star

Your behavior is repeatedly
Exhausting. One minute, I'm
Longing for your vapor, your atmosphere,
But, again, you prove that you
Burn all

That enters your world to be.
Claims come from your surface
That you are not like Mercury or
Jupiter. Your orbit is a singular
Loop. Yet, you lap more and more.

You are there, never warning me
As you appear in the early sky.

June 5, 2018

Character

My author, I guess,
Finds it compelling
To twist my arc

With nonsensical emotions.
The adjectives my author
Uses must be pompous.

O, the way my author
Plots me is with shock
Value—dumb, intelligent

Motives. What drives the
Way I am written? How
Is it that I've spent

Paragraphs detailing minor,
Minor fantasies? My author delays
Catharsis often and well.

April 25, 2018

Trapezoids are Triangular Squares

The scent of coffee watered words for me;
I giggled at triangular stories:
Their edges, their corners, their enhancement.

His voice—shared measurements—ate the cafe.
Those around could never match his struggle.
I found care that day in a mood-lit room,

But yet a woman, sharing our full space
Analyzed the differences between us:
She, her squared eyes, fell flat on our tri-backs.

July 17, 2018

Bowling

The woman,
Her hair silver,
Dominates ten again.

They cheer.
Her team, that is.
She bats her hand,

O, it's nothing,
She must think,
Ten after ten, an average

Like perfection.
And her peers, their hair
All aged, give her awe,

Encouragement.
Their power, their strikes
All built with plural and equal charge.

June 3, 2018

Little Boy Daydreams

He gave voices to the kids
Who didn't talk to him,
And inside this fabricated reality,

He and his team saved the world.

The trouble was,
That despite his imagination
Creating the story,

He was unable to

Change a dark demon
That haunted his thirst,
His teeth, and his jaw.

168

The world he was included in
Still had a flaw.

However, in this daydream,
His adapted friends gave
Him care, making

Sure, he made it through
The blood-craving disease.

They were there for him,
Even when he couldn't
Sleep.

May 29, 2018

Static; To Carry On

Fuck,

July 18, 2018

Conflict Lately

What is this rare inside?
Why must I feel as though
The common is my tied?

Rare breaks at the edges,
Streaming juices inward.
Sip, sip, sip, orgasm

Straight from the spoken word.
Fear the shallow basin
Where I drink romance, slurred.

"Doubt, doubt, doubt trust given,"
I hear the common shout!
Can't I be forgiven?

Can't I strangle through past
And only see glory?
I long for days I feel

Hope and a whole story.
I tire of dwelling,
Get me past this yelling.

July 6, 2018

Bathe

The edges around my drifting area
Are large with blankets. I let my hands
Drip across the surface,
And I wonder where I have gone.

The soap lathers against my youth
Skin, and I feel my chest tense. I am
Floating above the drowning area,
A place that I have visited often

These past few weeks. It is textured
With poison bubbles and promiscuous
Pleasures. I beckon and my voice does
Not echo. So, I slip my fingertips over

My shoulder once more. The water is
Cold. I wonder (with such sink) if my
Toes will dip down under to a place
Where I can be free of all these bathing salts.

November 28, 2017

Brush

Soft bumps slip across
My front teeth and I can
Feel the chocolate I ate
This morning. Disintegration.

There is a city. It lives.
Its people are the flavors
For which I don't wash
Away. They live.

They whisper to me,
They do. They tell me not
To banish them from their
Lovely settlement—to let live.

I pack my bags. My stuff.
My crap. My litter for which I last.
The train for which I'll disappear
Will be here soon and I will

Part to them—my flavors.
They'll welcome me well.
I can feel their glee—
Lunch's forgiveness, Dinner's remembrance.

My twine will come undone,
And I'll slip across the yellows,
Dancing with only them. Escaping
My lost hair. I know it so.

November 20, 2017

Paper Tied into a Notebook

My knowledge of it
Was eraser marks on white—
It had been scuffed quite often,
With its front

And back lead-grey. They
Were phrases for which
It heard, moments I can never
Be aware. As I know now,

I couldn't have known then
That parchment blends into
Art—ink being kept
Without second thought.

One day, I was mere
Invisible marks; months later,
I was informed of scribbles
And their counterparts.

April 4, 2018

Locomotion

Dwelling on the past hours,
I see its dragon eyes in my
Rear-view mirror.

We were a trio of heroes
Climbing the mountain of
Gold in its cave.

Verbally, we laid out the adventure
As it came.
And, though, its engine roared,

We hollered back,
And it came tumbling
Onto our sword.

We gobbled its treasure,
Laughing.
We were three separate legends,

And I was there to share
The same tale,
Anticipating the consumption of diamonds.

June 30, 2018

He's Dead Now

Filtration of those lousy bogs:
I watch them bud into flowers,
Growing over corpses of frogs.

O, I pick and pick through soft earth.
My fingers decompose tonight,
Concentrating on a stillbirth.

Its tiny arms are limp and cold.
I exhale silk-life to its lungs,
Gifting citrus wake. (I am told.)

Like times before, it dies again,
And I watch and weep to dismay.
(The quiet curse of failed semen.)

Soon, I become a traveler,
Searching for that eccentric branch:
O, wondrous leaves and between.

Get me far from this tame infant,
My drowsy wishes to dance now.
It's all my mental will allow.

July 21, 2018

Acceptance

Settle,
Do not waste teeth
Speaking complaints
About the subjects
That seem unjust.

Wash in the tide
Of the things to come,
Backside atop the crusted sand.
That is purely why consciousness
Was gifted: for flesh to be soaked.

Imminent, unavoidable,
Listen to the words.
Silent the pulsing breath.
Awakening is but letting the typewriter
Continue on without finger.

Human
Life is filled with
Moments that cannot be helped,
And cannot be overcome
. . . ?

July 3, 2018

My Writing Hand

Their teeth shred through the
Canyons on the palm. Surely,
They think a task would
Never be acceptable, never
possible. But it is this
Limb that produces their fears.

March 21, 2018

Time Interloper

V

Scattered, a man in a violet spacesuit
Found himself in many history books.
He was here, there, and all decades indeed.

Time, with one last effort, plotted a way
To remove this cavity from *Her* stream:
By luring him well with false inclusion.

Beyond the outer limits, there was space,
Friendship, and other small and scared people.
A place to be, something to fill his greed.

Their unreal kindness was enough to trap
Him once and for all. There, *Time* unraveled
His body—this man led by illusion,

Now chunks of soft flesh, all torn and blasted,
Time swept his incarnations from *Her* plate:
Not an interloper, but outcasted.

May 23, 2018

Tattoo

Speckled, spotted, my hands have haunted
Me since childhood. They grow to
Depths for which no one can match.
The sun attempts to ink my fingers,
It fails, it glides, and it seizes.

"You'll have to live with it,"
They say of the new adapted,
Gifted, addition for myself. Please,
Know it's not for dumb, adolescent
Aesthetic, no, it is my printed

Stories, emotions, and experiences
All spilled out on my wrist. I have
Lived with my body, my horrid
Skin. Let me bleed, let me see
My cognition on my being.

May 10, 2018

Educate Me on Mint Ice Cream

There's a lost stone within this bowl.
Spoonful after each, I imagine I must be close.
Don't tell me to pause,

I am a warrior, consuming the cold of filthy sin.
You are Atlas, below the great neon basin,
Feel as my stomach coils in the moon rain.

Soon, I will be there, unable to crunch down on dirt,
It will be mighty; your legs are patching! Cement dusting.
Wait. My jaws may be frozen, but I am almost there!

July 18, 2018

Busy Day

Why am I compelled to milk ambition?
I know not the length I will go, to when
I will stop. I feed on treats that I find,

Gaining piles of gold—overworked—this
Gleam, it drives me to heights of great torture.
This feat, its blood, I drink with my earth mind.

April 27, 2018

Anagnorisis

My eyes feel as though
They are dead flesh
Living in my skull.

O, my sleep prior was haunted with every
Word that has ever been spoken to me.
Who knew days still lived up there? In that

Cavern of suppression and unilluminated shadows,
That wooden pathway in the damp forest. We many
Live there—or at least I have formed you that way,

That tired, old, repetitive life you must live in that cave.
Obsession paints the walls with that of prehistoric
Humans killing beasts and strange ideas of what it is like

To live in a world where there are not rock entrapments.
Hours after the moment of my wanting sleep, I was given
Way to the men who wander there. They lashed at the

196

Miniscule exit: The way where false light shines.
I am eaten by my hubris, by my infatuation with what
Could have been. The trees, the sediment, they

Give voice to my ideas. The reality of the forest
Is that the woodlands have not told me such things.
It is my echo that builds a foundation for these ghosts.

The foliage must be annoyed by my frights, my transparent
Stockings of sounds for which I think I hear. We cavemen
Do yell back; it is the reverberation that hollows the trunks.

June 13, 2018

Repetitive Nature

I come from the sky. I hit the blacktop onward
Before a boy—a boy who sits and watches
With his thumb bleeding. (His cat scratched him.)
I form a shifting

Ground-cloud for him to enjoy as I waltz
Through the uneven earth, pavement that
Has been traced over by cars and feet.
I am a single-thought, lasting only the

Lifetime of gravity. (Taking in all that I can:)
O, the vast land, I can see all trees from here,
In the open, where my siblings no longer
Block my view. And yet this slips by, my

Duty to the roots is a faint call. I obey. The
Larger-than-life life, it rises past my
Personified ears. I can't have that single
Thought: the fall. My vision is a falsification

Of a boy who is merely distracted by the
Bugs that shift (continuously) inside of me.
How can that be? I haven't a clue, nor can he.
I'm merely the sky, and then the ground.

I can't know the observation my fellow kin make,
I can't know my kin before me. It is our mission,
To target and slap against that rock, those leaves, and
The face of a bloodied-thumb boy.

May 21, 2018

Walking Home

Waxing behind a fantastic fabric,
You hide so obviously from sight.
Your figure hangs proud above
The nearing buildings, and I finger

The glass air, unable to comprehend
How your fine-shaped body is so defined,
So cut-out. Not as if you were shaded, but
Actually paper, sliced with great intention,

Then masked in thick, white gas—hung
Above us all, only to watch as we party
Your realm thin. Mute, you are the gazing
Light that is constant, clear, and loud.

April 20, 2018

Finite

The dam, beyond to my left, must be washing so fiery in
    the dark.
Their malleable souls play hopscotch along its center. I
    listen with wet
Intentions; my eyes coax themselves into lust for the
    surrounding environment.

This must be among the many beginnings of the closing
    chapters. Words with hollow
Meaning strike our conversations on repeat. O, this
    invisible dam prances in the
Light showers. The sky, its ten o'clock shadow; their
    mouths, the three of them

Laughing. My shoes are frightened of the mud, the way it
    intimidates the boogeyman.
Minutes earlier, I was consuming a sandwich which spoke
    of dry gas station flavors:
Forgettable, a filler, a waste of my fuel. Damn, be the
    young few that swim in air,

I am only one of this jigsaw, this magnetic simplification
    of desire. We were only
Drawn here for my adoration to the saddening ceiling. It
    is darkening around the
Edges, where leaks escape toward my right. The boys,
    they don't notice how the

Above collapses, at least not when I stare up to see the
    telephone wires, all shimmering
In the distant street lamps. Dimensional beings must
    probe my sockets all too often.
They receive several opportunities with their subtle kisses;
    daggers, if one will. I

Cut my face open every time I look upon them, up there,
    where I cannot see.
Down here, though, the visuals are saturated with
    undefined secrets. We, us
Three, do lick our eyelids, and we are gone the next day.
    Our farewells are

Driven and drawn in such minute detail. The overlapping
    globe does not care
To focus on us in the moments after, only *I* sense the
    river, its cleansing of the
Encompassing trees. Then, it is tomorrow, and my ears
    only taste words which

Feel like muffled shouts under feet of water. These are
    the stanzas I don't soak
In well enough, at least not well enough to remember the
    full current: the todays
And the tomorrows, the quick things I wish away too
    soon, the rainy, rainy nights.

May 9, 2018

Freshman

I

That hotel was painted with smoke,
I can't quite say now if it was the same,
For I visited often,

But I knew one of the buildings had a stench
Of past humans roaming around.

(Pause for sleep,)
I drew in leaf-infested air,
They left me there.

Again,
Obviously, I knew I would see them
Once more, but what is change

But knives in the neck?

(Pause, again.)

We were all lily pads,
Frozen atop a surface together,
Meeting and binding our greens.

Unlike the usual, however,
From there I grew branches.

(They would return,
I woke every morning,
And I said they would come

Back. I wasn't going to be
Tethered forever.)

We were to become
Omnipotent plants.
Just not yet.

II

A show
Of unfamiliarity
Strung up with

People
That had hidden
Details, unseen by me.

We complained—
As all great theater does.

We danced with acting
That would be exposition
To later inserts of scenes.

III

Three great
Events all hung
Me by a belt,

My throbbing esophagus
Could never take hold
Of the infatuation that fled

From my eyes.

One: I was given
A great, great soul part,
Birthed from

A time of writers
That I could not see,

Two: A past event
Had toppled down with
The chair, and struck me

Quite strangled, slapped me around,
A voice for which I knew no other,
Sung harmonious to another,

And I was dangling,
My toes touching the carpet,
But swinging and grazing a

Yellow curtain. Songs have a special
Way of murder, they do.

Three: I met a wicked
Tree with roots so strong,
They lifted me up briefly,

In this sandstorm mess.

IV

A doctoral-made monster was me.
They removed my neck,
And I became a plant without

Trunk, begging for the flowing of
Life, a stream I could drink from.

That given soul reflected so well,
Not even my acting could stop
A fresh repetitive hell from grasping

My chin and choking what was left.

V

I hoped the fertilization
From the tree's roots
Would gain me some,

I was wrong,

Not even I,
The writer,
Could alter a past

I did not invent.

Though,
I did witness the
Voice thrice more,

And my digestive
Tracks rotted from the inside
Out.

Growth was beyond me.

VI

Internally,
I never
belonged.

I cast myself
To horizons
That blurred with

Dark suns.

(Pause.)

Those two voices
Floated on their own,
Without my sight.

I thought about it
Often.

(Pause again.)

The flares gave way
Through my frontal,
And I broke out,

Sobbing out onto
My lower hand,

The connection
Was to my veins.

VII

That voice again,
Damn the demon
And its motives,

What kind of hideous beast
Has such elegant vocals?

My outcast salvia
struggled to limp away,

The twisted tree and a fellow
Water pad aided my getaway.

Together, we ate wallpaper,
Peeling and creeping round
The room's ends.

My fellow nature items
Told me of how they gnawed
On walls' surfaces previous.

The pad, however,
Began not that long
ago.

Here I was thinking
They were static,
And existed

Purely as I met them.

VIII

The penultimate
was filled with
a final

show. It was *filled*
With the usual hate,
A new sense of

Belonging.

(Pause.)

The ponds I swam in
Were gone, I was situated
In a lake.

And up, my body went,
Festering out into a whole
That shaded the ground.

Squirrels lived
In my many rooms.

One, with the fuzziest of tails,
I had seen in side hills
(over yonder).

He was more than
Acorns. A rodent that could
Play humor with beautiful tunes,

A mammal with caramel
Seeping from its ears.

Candy makes siblings, too,
I suppose.

IX

In the center of
Development,
Those around me

Were still so fresh
After winter left us
Wet.

They were all buildings
Attempting to not show
That they were haunted by spirits.

I touched their jagged
Stairs and knew
All scents

That lived within.

(They returned, sometime later,)
I never got to share
Their estate for much longer,

Soon, though.

May 15, 2018

To Be Different

Imagination, when it be trapped tight,
Cannot fathom the possibilities
Of being something other than what's right,
What's static, and what's one's abilities.
Its limited state will be the cause of fright,
Horror, having seen abnormalities.

To be different, though, is to know motion,
To know running, and hiding, and pleading.
Those who are fixed, know not the mere notion
Of being behind those who are leading.
We shifting *many* among commotion
Will be ones that stand above misreading.

Tired of the constant one-motion sea,
We progress shall be the ones that are free.

May 29, 2018

Time's End

It was not the first star, it was the last.
And *She* was there for its birth and its death,
Guiding its story through each potential.

She spoke—uttered—every important thought.
All stories, once the last light went out, told.
O, this was *Her* narrative concluded.

And amongst *Her* hums as everything closed,
She thought of *Space's* nebulous fingers
Massaging all that was quite essential.

Mimicked motion, knowing it to be gone,
Her songs became distress to the silent.
In flirting, forever was alluded,

But here *She* was without *His* faint kissing.
Lies and insults separated them both.
As the dark seeped in, nothing was missing.

June 30, 2018

Acknowledgements

Thank you

> to Grace Roberts for the beautiful cover art.

> to Ryan Wilson for reading all of my works.

> to Ryan Smet for editing and forming this collection of poetry.

> to friends who have stayed with me.

> to family who have supported me in my writing.

> to *you* for taking the time to join the *Interloper* on his journey.

> I hope your travels are safe.

Index

www.ingramcontent.com/pod-product-compliance
Lightning Source LLC
Chambersburg PA
CBHW072137090426
42739CB00013B/3212